D1091698

Sacraments etchings:
Lorenzo Zucchi after Giuseppe Maria Crespi, 1765.

SAINTS *and* SACRAMENTS

Companion book to
The Sacraments Study Program

PEGGY PANDALEON

WORD ON FIRE CATHOLIC MINISTRIES
www.WORDONFIRE.org

CONTENTS

FOREWORD

When the Church canonizes someone, it declares that the person "practiced heroic virtue and lived in fidelity to God's grace," according to the *Catechism*.[1] We all receive a special and guaranteed outpouring of God's grace each time we receive a sacrament in faith and love. The saints all cooperated with the grace of the Holy Spirit in order to follow and accomplish the unique mission that God entrusted to each one of them. Each one of us has a unique mission as well and needs the grace of the sacraments, along with all other forms of grace, to walk the path God has prepared especially for us and follow the universal call to holiness.

To bring life and depth to the discussion of the sacraments, this book highlights one saint for each sacrament. Each chosen saint personifies a certain sacrament by the words and deeds of their earthly lives. From St. Francis Xavier, the Jesuit who baptized more people than anyone in history, to St. Maximillian Kolbe, the Franciscan priest who offered his own life as a sacrifice to save a fellow prisoner in Auschwitz, these seven saints model surrender to Christ and a sure path to holiness. They truly are living signs of the power of God's grace that flows through the sacraments.

1   *Catechism of the Catholic Church*, no. 828

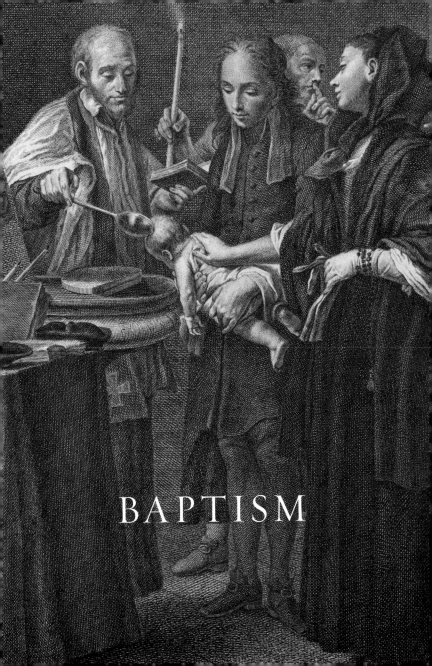

BAPTISM

BAPTISM
St. Francis Xavier

God chose St. Francis Xavier to baptize more people than possibly anyone in the history of the Church. St. Francis Xavier didn't plan to be a missionary, or even a Jesuit, but God led him to those roles because he had a very specific mission in mind for him. Francis Xavier brought tens of thousands of people on the distant continent of Asia to Christ and his Church. How many did he baptize? Estimates range anywhere between thirty thousand and seven hundred thousand—and his missionary work lasted only ten short years!

At the "mother church" of the Society of Jesus (the Jesuits), the Church of the Gesu in Rome, there is only one relic on display from Francis Xavier. His well-preserved right hand and forearm has been there for centuries, raised in testimony to the powerful sacrament that he conferred on countless Asians.

Growing up in a wealthy family in the Basque region of Spain, Francis Xavier had planned to devote his life to the Church as a theologian. In 1525, he left Spain to attend the University of Paris, the theological and intellectual center of Europe at the time, to begin his studies. Francis roomed with another Basque student, Ignatius of Loyola, who was fifteen years older and had experienced a life-changing religious conversion. Ignatius gathered a group of like-minded men who shared his faith and his ideals, gradually winning over the initially reluctant Francis Xavier. Each member of the group participated in a rudimentary version of what later became Ignatius' *Spiritual Exercises*, a series of practices and meditations designed to strengthen the interior life and guide one to greater service of God. The *Exercises* inspired Francis Xavier to devote his life entirely to the Lord. In 1534, this band of seven men took vows of poverty and chastity. They initially desired to travel to the Holy Land and work for the conversion of the Muslims living there, but their plan was thwarted by the Turkish wars. They went instead to Rome, and six years later, in September 1540, Pope Paul III approved their request to establish a new religious order, the Society of Jesus. They pledged their obedience to the pope "for the good of souls," offering to go wherever he would send them.

Initially, the pope enlisted their services in Italy. They quickly attracted the attention of King John III of Portugal, who sought priests to support the Christians and to evangelize the peoples in his new Asian territories, principally in India. Two priests were chosen to undertake the mission but when one fell ill, Francis Xavier was chosen to take his place.

In March 1540, Francis Xavier left Rome for Lisbon and, after a brief stint in Portuguese Mozambique, he then sailed to Goa, India. He carried the title of Papal Nuncio to the East, acting as a diplomat to the region for the Holy Father. During their thirteen-month voyage to India, Francis Xavier took all on board under his spiritual care. He preached on deck every Sunday, offered catechism to the crew, settled quarrels, and cared for the sick. The ship landed in Goa, the epicenter of Portuguese colonial activity, in May 1542.

The Portuguese had been in Goa for thirty years, but the practice of the Catholic faith had fallen off significantly. They did not live out their faith and set a poor moral example for the Indian people. One of the biggest scandals was the taking of concubines from among the native women. Francis Xavier sought to correct the situation with methods that were sensible, humane, and tactful, thereby earning the respect of all.

Francis Xavier was known to be very charismatic with a "dashing and robust personality" and was also described as "joyful," "practical," "prudent," "creative," "astounding," and "decisive." Francis Xavier understood people. He worked tirelessly to learn each native language where he ministered, wearing the indigenous dress and eating the food of the peoples to establish a closer connection.

A companion of Francis Xavier described him in this way: "I have never met anyone more filled with faith and hope, more open-minded than Francis. He never seems to lose his great joy and enthusiasm. He talks to both the good and the bad. Anything he is asked to do, Francis does willingly, simply because he loves everyone."[1]

Francis Xavier described his work in one of the many letters he sent back to the Jesuit headquarters in Rome:

In this region of Travancore, where I now am, God has drawn very many to the faith of His Son Jesus Christ. In the space of one month I made Christians of more than ten thousand. This is the method I have followed. As soon as I arrived in any heathen village where they had sent for me to give them baptism, I gave orders for all, men, women, and children, to be collected in one place. Then, beginning with the first elements of the Christian faith, I taught them there is one God—Father, Son, and Holy Ghost; and at the same time, calling on the three divine persons and One God, I made them each make three times the sign of the Cross; then, putting on a surplice, I began to recite in a loud voice and in their own language the form of general

Confession, the Apostles' Creed, the Ten Commandments, the Lord's Prayer, the Ave Maria, and the Salve Regina. Two years ago I translated all these prayers into the language of the country, and learned them by heart. I recited them so that all of every age and condition followed me in them. Then I began to explain shortly the articles of the Creed and the Ten Commandments in the language of the country. Where the people appeared to me sufficiently instructed to receive baptism, I ordered them all to ask God's pardon publicly for the sins of their past life, and to do this with a loud voice and in the presence of their neighbors still hostile to the Christian religion, in order to touch the hearts of the heathen and confirm the faith of the good. They willingly hear about the mysteries and rules of the Christian religion, and treat me, poor sinner as I am, with the greatest respect. Many, however, put away from them with hardness of heart the truth which they well know. When I have done my instruction, I ask one by one all those who desire baptism if they believe without hesitation each of the articles of the faith. All immediately, holding their arms in the form of the Cross, declare with one voice that they believe all entirely. Then at last I baptize them in due form, and I give to each his name written on a ticket. After their baptism the new Christians go back to their houses and bring me their wives and families for baptism. When all are baptized, I order all the temples of their false gods to be destroyed and all the idols to be broken in pieces. I can give you no idea of the joy I feel in seeing this done, witnessing the destruction of the idols by the very people who but lately adored them. In all the towns and villages I leave the Christian doctrine in writing in the language of the country, and I prescribe at the same time the manner in which it is to be taught in the morning and evening schools. When I have done all this in one place, I pass to another, and so on successively to the rest. In this way I go all round the country, bringing the natives into the fold of Jesus Christ, and the joy that I feel in this is far too great to be expressed in a letter, or even by word of mouth.[2]

In Travancore, where he penned the above letter, he established forty-five churches and was called "The Great Father." Miracles of healing often occurred in the poor villages he visited. Unlike many missionaries over the centuries, Francis Xavier didn't just baptize and move on. He ensured that there was someone left in each new Christian community to continue catechesis, even asking Rome for new recruits to come and staff the churches he had established. He wrote to Ignatius:

Many, many people hereabouts are not becoming Christians for one reason: there is nobody to make them Christians. Again and again I have thought of going round the universities of Europe, especially Paris, and everywhere crying out like a madman. Riveting the attention of those with more learning than charity: "What a tragedy: how many souls are being shut out of heaven and falling into hell, thanks to you!" I wish they would work as hard at this as they do at their books, and so settle their account with God for their learning and the talents entrusted to them.[3]

Francis Xavier did well with the common people, even teaching key tenets of the faith to the children in rhyme and song, so that they could go home and sing them to their families. He did not fare as well with the officials, only converting one high-caste Brahmin in a year's time. Often, he was violently opposed, and his enemies attempted to burn down his hut while he was inside. On another occasion, he saved his life only by hiding from his pursuers in the branches of a large tree.

After spending seven years in India and the Malay Peninsula, Francis Xavier learned of the existence of the islands of Japan. The fact that there were still new worlds without knowledge of Christ motivated him. He is quoted as saying, "I want to be where there are out-and-out pagans," and one of his favorite prayers was "Give me souls!" Francis Xavier set about learning the Japanese language, which he said was the most difficult of all.

In Japan, Francis Xavier had to change his approach. The Emperor of the first province he visited would never receive or listen to someone dressed in the rags he usually wore, so

Francis Xavier changed into elegant clothing and brought gifts, thereby winning the Emperor's friendship and opening up a new opportunity to preach the Gospel. He was given free rein to preach in the province and even given residence at a deserted Buddhist temple.

He came to realize that the way to further conversion in Japan must proceed through China, since the Japanese looked to China for wisdom. The Chinese government prohibited entrance to their country by foreigners, but Francis Xavier worked creatively and tirelessly with local merchants and his companions to reach China anyway. Unfortunately, he died trying. St. Francis Xavier succumbed to fever on December 3, 1552, on an island just off the Chinese coast.

Not yet knowing of his death, Ignatius wrote to Francis Xavier a few weeks later to recall him to Europe as his successor as head of the Society of Jesus. This gives us a clear sense of the high esteem that Ignatius had for Francis Xavier. Ignatius of Loyola and Francis Xavier were canonized together in 1622. In 1927, Pope Pius XI named St. Francis Xavier the official co-patron of foreign missions (along with St. Thérèse of Lisieux).

The areas the saint evangelized in India have remained Catholic to the present day. The missions he founded on the Malay Peninsula and in Japan were destroyed in the seventeenth century through violent and prolonged persecution. But the faith there did not go quietly, as thousands who traced their faith to Francis Xavier and his companions were martyred for their devotion to Christ.

St. Francis Xavier's feast day is December 3.

St. Francis Xavier, pray for us that we may bring the love, truth, and goodness of Christ to all who do not know him.

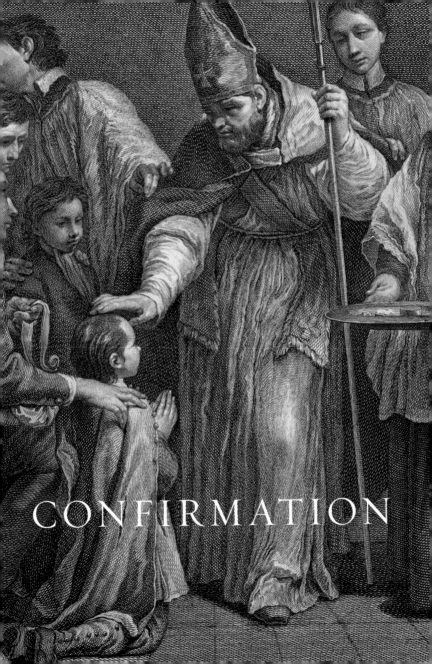

CONFIRMATION

CONFIRMATION
St. John Paul II

There is little doubt that the best contemporary example of an authentic, public, and very effective "soldier of Christ" was St. John Paul II. He is credited with helping to defeat Communism in Eastern Europe and with re-evangelizing the universal Church in face of the onslaught of secularism that threatened the faith in the last half of the twentieth century and into the new millennium.

St. John Paul II truly personifies the sacrament of Confirmation, which, as the *Catechism of the Catholic Church* puts it, "gives us a special strength of the Holy Spirit to spread and defend the faith by word and action as true witnesses of Christ" (CCC, no. 1303).[4] Or, as Bishop Barron says in the film, a "special force of the Holy Spirit." St. John Paul II was a *special force* indeed, one empowered and emboldened by the grace of the Holy Spirit and fully resplendent with the gifts of the Spirit, which he used as a priest, and in his office as pope, to bring Christ more fully into the world.

Born Karol Wojtyla in Wadowice, Poland, on May 18, 1920, he experienced much sorrow at a young age, losing his mother at age nine, his brother at twelve, and his father at twenty. After high school, he started at the Jagiellonian University of Krakow, but the Nazis closed the university a year later in 1939, so he worked in a quarry and chemical factory from 1940–1944.

Discerning a call to the priesthood, he began secretly studying at the Krakow seminary in 1942. During that time, he and a few friends formed the Rhapsodic Theatre and met secretly, usually at night, to recite by candlelight the great works of Polish literature, which the Nazis had banned. Bishop Barron writes, "The Rhapsodic Theatre was doing much more than preserving the Polish language and culture, because an inescapable ingredient in the plays and poems they loved was Catholicism. To read Polish literature was to remember God, creation, the fall, the prophets of Israel, the Incarnation, the redemption, the cross, eternal life, and the irreducible dignity of the human being."[5] Wojtyla was keeping the faith alive in a dark and oppressive time.

After the war ended, Wojtyla completed his theological studies and was ordained in 1946. After a few years of advanced study in Rome, he served as a parish priest in Krakow, where he often led groups of students on hiking, skiing, bicycling, camping, and kayaking trips, accompanied by prayer, outdoor Masses, and theological discussions. In Stalinist-era Poland, it was not permitted for priests to travel with groups of students; consequently, Wojtyla asked his younger companions to call him "Wujek" (Polish for "Uncle") to prevent outsiders from knowing he was a priest. The nickname stuck with him in Poland for the rest of his life.

Later, while teaching ethics at Jagiellonian University and subsequently at the Catholic University of Lublin, Wojtyla gathered a group of students to meet for prayer, philosophical discussion, and to help serve the blind and the sick. Starting with about twenty young adults who called themselves *Rodzinka*, the "little family," the group eventually grew to about 200 members. At age thirty-eight, Wojtyla became the youngest bishop ever ordained in Poland.

Young people, not far from the age of having received the sacrament of Confirmation, always seemed to gravitate to Wojtyla. As pope, he prioritized his special love for young people by establishing World Youth Day. The largest single gathering in Christian history was the Manila World Youth Day in 1995, with estimates of over four million attendees.

John Paul II presided over nine World Youth Days during his papacy. The first was in Rome in 1986. The bold evangelical theme of the first gathering encouraged the confirmed to "Always be ready to make your defense to anyone who demands from you an accounting for the hope that is in you" (1 Peter 3:15). Always exhorting young people to remain faithful and find their purpose in the Lord, he said at World Youth Day in 2000:

It is Jesus in fact that you seek when you dream of happiness; he is waiting for you when nothing else you find satisfies you; he is the beauty to which you are so attracted; it is he who provokes you with that thirst for fullness that will not let you settle for compromise; it is he who urges you to shed the masks of a false life; it is he who reads in your hearts your most genuine choices, the choices that others try to stifle.[6]

In Toronto in 2002, John Paul II's last World Youth Day, he said this to the eight hundred thousand gathered with him:

When, back in 1985, I wanted to start the World Youth Days . . . I imagined [them] as a *powerful moment* in which the young people of the world could meet Christ, who is eternally young, and could learn from him how to be *bearers of the Gospel to other young people.* This evening, together with you, I praise God and give thanks to him for the gift bestowed on the Church through the World Youth Days. Millions of young people have taken part, and as a result have become better and more committed Christian witnesses.[7]

Truly, his leadership was a *special force* for reminding the confirmed of their role as "soldiers of Christ."

John Paul II served one of the longest papal terms, spanning almost 27 years from 1978 to 2005. No other pope met as many people or traveled as far and wide as he did. Leading the Church's evangelization efforts from the top, John Paul II visited 129 countries, logging more than 680,000 miles, during his pontificate. As the Apostles spoke to all the assembled nationalities at the first Pentecost, he could also be heard speaking many languages, having learned twelve and using nine during his papacy.

All who believe in Christ should feel, as an integral part of their faith, an apostolic concern to pass on to others its light and joy. This concern must become, as it were, a hunger and thirst to make the Lord known, given the vastness of the non-Christian world.[8]

Due in large part to his influence, Communism in Poland and the rest of Europe was defeated with minimal conflict. In June 1979, shortly after he was elected pope, John Paul II returned to Poland and celebrated Mass in Warsaw with hundreds of thousands of people and the entire Polish Communist government watching. In his homily, he spoke of God, "of freedom, and of human rights—all topics frowned on by the Communist regime," writes Bishop Barron. "As the pope preached, the people began to chant, 'We want God; we want God; we want God.' The chant did not stop for an astonishing fifteen minutes. It is said that during this demonstration of the people's will, John Paul turned toward the Polish government officials and gestured, as if to say, 'Do you hear?'"[9] Insightful observers recognized that Communism was basically dead in Poland after the pope's visit, and in fact, it collapsed across all of Europe only a few years later.

After an attempt was made on Pope John Paul II's life in St. Peter's Square on May 13, 1981, he forgave his would-be assassin, following Christ's call to forgive one's enemies. This attack did not deter his efforts to evangelize. In fact, he courageously and generously intensified his pastoral commitments, realizing that his life was spared so he could go on being a "soldier of Christ."

He fought valiantly for the dignity of every human being and for the right to life from conception to natural death. In what is possibly his most important and relevant encyclical for our times, *Evangelium Vitae* ("The Gospel of Life"), he boldly proclaimed the Church's teachings on the sanctity of human life and condemned the evils of murder, abortion, and euthanasia, while also denouncing the use of capital punishment, except in cases of "absolute necessity . . . when it would not be possible otherwise to defend society."[10]

> We are facing an enormous and dramatic clash between good and evil, death and life, the "culture of death" and the "culture of life." We find ourselves not only "faced with" but necessarily "in the midst of" this conflict: we are all involved and we all share in it, with the inescapable responsibility of choosing to be unconditionally pro-life.[11]

To ensure that the faithful had a ready reference for Catholic teachings and could really understand their faith, John Paul II commissioned the writing of a new universal catechism. In 1992, John Paul promulgated the *Catechism of the Catholic Church*. He described the publication as a "a sure norm for teaching the faith . . . [and] a sure and authentic reference text for teaching Catholic doctrine and particularly for preparing local catechisms."[12]

As a prolific writer, teacher, and defender of the faith, Pope John Paul II left a permanent legacy with fourteen encyclicals, fifteen apostolic exhortations, and many apostolic constitutions and apostolic letters. He also wrote several books during his papacy, including: *Crossing the Threshold of Hope* (1994); *Gift and Mystery: On the Fiftieth Anniversary of My Priestly Ordination* (1996); *Roman Triptych* (2003); *Rise, Let Us Be on Our Way* (2004); and *Memory and Identity* (2005).

Pope John Paul II died in the Vatican on April 2, 2005, the vigil of Divine Mercy Sunday, a feast that he had instituted. He was canonized on April 27, 2014, by Pope Benedict XVI, his immediate successor.

St. John Paul II's feast day is October 22.

St. John Paul II, pray for us that we may live out our Confirmation duty to bring the Gospel of hope and love to all we meet.

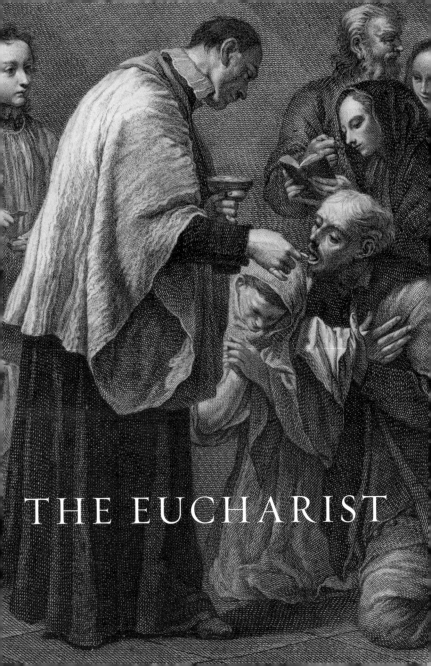

THE EUCHARIST

THE EUCHARIST
St. Clare of Assisi (and all saints)

To say that only one saint best exemplifies devotion to the Eucharist is to say that only one saint best worships Jesus Christ. Impossible! Saints are holy due to their conformity to Christ, and the surest way on earth to become like Christ is to partake of his Body and Blood often. To, so to speak, become what you eat.

One saint that not only adored and received the Eucharist as often as possible, but used its power to fight evil, was St. Clare of Assisi. "The Miracle of the Eucharist of Assisi" speaks to the Real Presence of Jesus in the Host, and his divine power over all things.

Emperor Frederick II of Sweden declared war against the pope and was trying to conquer territory from Assisi down to Sicily. He recruited an army of ruthless Saracen mercenaries and advanced toward Assisi in 1241. The army was stationed outside the convent of San Damiano and began to put ladders up against the walls, preparing to overtake the convent as it lay in the path to the rest of the city. In terror, the women of the Order of Poor Ladies ran to their Mother Superior, St. Clare, for help.

St. Clare was ill in bed, so two nuns helped her up and brought her into the convent chapel to get the Blessed Sacrament. She held the monstrance in her arms, pressed her head against it, and prayed: "Doth it please Thee, my Lord, to deliver Thy defenceless handmaids, whom I have nourished with Thy love, into the hands of the pagans? Defend O Lord, I beseech Thee, these Thy servants who I in this hour am unable to defend." A very sweet, childlike voice answered, "I will always defend thee." Clare added another prayer. "My Lord . . . if it please Thee protect the city, for it supporteth us for love of Thee." Christ replied, "It will be troubled, but it shall be defended by My protection." She comforted the sisters: "Rest assured, I bid you, little daughters, that ye shall suffer no harm; only trust in Christ."[13]

Then Clare, raising her face covered with tears, held the monstrance up before an open window facing the army in the convent courtyard below. Gazing at the monstrance as if seeing the Lord God himself, the army retreated back over the walls in fear. The people of Assisi were astonished that the Saracens had not attacked their city. The invaders fled without setting one foot in the town.

From childhood, St. Clare was devoted to Christ in the Eucharist with a faith nurtured and supported by St. Francis of Assisi, who was twelve years her senior. She was born into nobility, a member of the Sciffi family. The families of Clare and Francis were connected, as both lived in Assisi, although Francis came from a successful but not noble merchant's family. Once, his mother sent Francis to the Sciffi castle with a healing remedy for Clare when she was three and ill with a fever.

When Lady Clare turned eighteen, her father informed her that a knight from Perugia was coming for her hand in marriage in a few short weeks. But Clare, who had been powerfully influenced by Francis' preaching of the Gospel and his love of poverty, asked him to shelter her, so she could devote her life entirely to Christ. One night, under the cover of darkness, she fled from her castle with her cousin Pacifica and was met by some of Francis' friars, who carried torches to light her way.

Francis cut Clare and Pacifica's hair, gave them veils, and took them to a nearby convent for safekeeping. A few days later, Clare's younger sister Agnes also ran away to join the convent. Clare's father was furious and tried to bring his daughters home, but his efforts were to no avail. As they clung to the altar, the girls told him they had now pledged their lives to God and to the poor.

Clare's Order of Poor Ladies grew; influenced by Clare and Pacifica, other noble ladies renounced their wealth and embraced a life of poverty. Clare was the first woman in Church history to write a rule of religious life for women. After her father's death, her mother, other sister, and aunt joined the convent. San Damiano, the small church that Francis had restored after hearing Jesus' voice from the cross, was transformed into a convent for the new order. The Order of Poor Ladies dedicated themselves to growing food for the poor and caring for the sick.

Sister Clare lived for many years after Francis' death and continued to carry on the Franciscan mission. She died in 1253 and was canonized two years later.

How great was Saint Clare's affection and devotion to the Sacrament of the Altar is shown by their effect. . . . When receiving the Body of the Lord, however, she at first shed burning tears and, approaching with trembling, she feared [Him who was] hidden in the Sacrament no less than [Him who was] ruling heaven and earth.[14]

She would take her disciple by the hand, lead her before Jesus lying on the straw at Bethlehem, blood-stained on the Cross, and veiled in the Eucharist, and say to her, "Look into your heart and search for the answer you will give Him."[15]

St. Clare's feast day is August 11.

St. Clare, pray for us that we might put all our trust in the Lord Jesus who changes our very beings through the Eucharist.

SAINTS *on* THE EUCHARIST

In honor of the importance of the Eucharist to *all* saints, here are some quotes and reflections from a few well-known saints:

"If angels could be jealous of men, they would be so for one reason: Holy Communion."[16] –St. Maximilian Kolbe

"You come to me and unite yourself intimately to me under the form of nourishment. Your blood now runs in mine, your soul, Incarnate God, compenetrates mine, giving courage and support. What miracles! Who would have ever imagined such!"[17] –St. Maximilian Kolbe

"The Blessed Sacrament is indeed the stimulus for us all, for me as it should be for you, to forsake all worldly ambitions. Without the constant presence of our Divine Master upon the altar in my poor chapels, I never could have persevered casting my lot with the lepers of Molokai, the foreseen consequences of which begins now to appear on my skin, and is felt throughout the body. The Holy Communion being the daily bread of a priest, I feel myself happy, well pleased, and resigned in the rather exceptional circumstance in which it has pleased Divine Providence to put me."[18]
–St. Damien of Molokai

"All good works together are not of equal value with the Sacrifice of the Mass, because they are the works of men, and the holy Mass is the work of God. Martyrdom is nothing in comparison; it is the sacrifice that man makes of his life to God; the Mass is the sacrifice that God makes to man of His Body and of His Blood."[19] —St. John Vianney

"When I am preparing for Holy Communion, I picture my soul as a piece of land and I beg the Blessed Virgin to remove from it *any rubbish* that would prevent it from being *free*; then I ask her to set up a huge tent worthy of *heaven*, adorning it with *her own jewelry*; finally, I invite all the angels and saints to come and conduct a magnificent concert there. It seems to me that when Jesus descends into my heart He is content to find Himself so well received and I, too, am content."[20] —St. Thérèse of Lisieux

"Let us take the time to kneel before Jesus present in the Eucharist, in order to make reparation by our faith and love for the acts of carelessness and neglect, and even the insults which our Savior must endure in many parts of the world. Let us deepen through adoration our personal and communal contemplation, drawing upon aids to prayer inspired by the word of God and the experience of so many mystics, old and new."[21] —St. John Paul II

"To evangelize the world there is need of apostles who are 'experts' in the celebration, adoration, and contemplation of the Eucharist."[22] –St. John Paul II

"Jesus has made Himself the bread of life to give us life. Night and day, he is there. If you really want to grow in love, come back to the Eucharist, come back to that adoration."[23] –St. Teresa of Kolkata

"Every morning during meditation, I prepare myself for the whole day's struggle. Holy Communion assures me that I will win the victory; and so it is. I fear the day when I do not receive Holy Communion. This Bread of the Strong gives me all the strength I need to carry on my mission and the courage to do whatever the Lord asks of me. The courage and strength that are in me are not of me, but of Him who lives in me—it is the Eucharist."[24] –St. Faustina

Jesus told St. Faustina: "I desire to unite Myself to human souls; My great delight is to unite Myself with souls. Know, My daughter, that when I come to a human heart in Holy Communion, My hands are full of all kinds of graces which I want to give to the soul. But souls do not even pay any attention to Me; they leave Me to Myself and busy themselves with other things. Oh, how sad I am that souls do not recognize Love! They treat Me as a dead object."[25]

RECONCILIATION

RECONCILIATION
St. John Vianney, Curé d'Ars

In an obscure part of the French countryside, in the little town of Ars, as many as twenty thousand pilgrims each year visited with the sole intent of having their confessions heard by Jean Marie Baptiste Vianney, the Curé d'Ars.

Spending twelve hours a day in the confessional in the winter, and up to eighteen hours in the summer, St. John Vianney labored to bring souls back into communion with God and the Church. He was blessed with the gift of "reading souls," which allowed him to identify sins that the penitent had forgotten or intentionally omitted, and also the gift of prophecy, which allowed him insight into future events in the lives of those whom he absolved. These gifts from God so impressed those who came for confession that they hung on his every word. He said little, but his few words were enough.

Once, St. John Vianney was asked how many serious sinners he had converted in one year, and he replied, "Seven hundred." A fellow pastor said, "Those of my parishioners who go to M. Vianney become models. I wish I could take my whole parish to him."[26]

Through the gifts of God, John Vianney could discern what spiritual barrier was troubling a person who was suffering. Once, a young girl came to him to ask that he cure her paralyzed leg. "My child," he told her, "you disobey your mother far too often, and answer her back in a disrespectful manner. If you wish the good God to cure you, you must correct that ugly defect. Oh! what a task lies before you! But remember one thing: you will indeed get well, but by degrees, according to how you try to correct that defect."[27] The girl returned home, resolving to show more respect to her mother. Her paralyzed leg, which had been four inches shorter than the other, started to grow longer, and in a few years, she was totally healed.

A cousin of St. John Vianney visited to ask prayers for one of her daughters who was very seriously ill. "She is ripe for Heaven," he said without hesitation. "As for you, my cousin, you need crosses to make you think of God."[28]

A poor girl who had become blind went with her mother on pilgrimage to Ars. St. John Vianney could sense her positive spirit and love of God. He told her, "My child, you can be cured, but if the good God restores your sight, your salvation will be less assured. If, on the contrary, you consent to keep your infirmity, you will go to Heaven, and I even guarantee that you will have a high place there."[29] The girl accepted his advice and no longer asked for a cure, perfectly resigned to God's will.

St. John Vianney's early life coincided with the anticlerical Reign of Terror phase of the French Revolution, when many priests were executed. As a result, he received catechesis for Confession and First Communion—and later the sacraments themselves—in secret. The bravery of priests and nuns who risked their lives for the sacraments made a deep impression on him. Soon, he felt called to the priesthood.

The French Revolution also interrupted his studies. He struggled as a student, particularly with Latin, for which he enlisted private tutoring. In 1802, the Catholic Church was reestablished in France, but John Vianney's ecclesiastical studies were cut short in 1809 when he was drafted into Napoleon Bonaparte's army. Two days into his service, he became ill and was hospitalized, while his troop continued on without him. Stopping to pray in a church, John Vianney met a young man who offered to reunite him with his troop, but then instead took him to a rural village full of deserters. He stayed until 1810, when amnesty was given for all deserters. He returned to the seminary, finished his ecclesiastical

Saints and Sacraments

studies, and was ordained in 1815. In 1818, he was assigned to a parish in the small village of Ars.

When he arrived in Ars, he found the townspeople very lukewarm in their Catholic faith and lax in their religious practices, most likely from the ravages of the French Revolution. He preached tirelessly in order to instill religious zeal in his parishioners:

> A lukewarm soul is not yet quite dead in the eyes of God because the faith, the hope, and the charity which are its spiritual life are not altogether extinct. But it is a faith without zeal, a hope without resolution, a charity without ardour. . . .

> Nothing touches this soul: it hears the word of God, yes, that is true; but often it just bores it. Any prayers which are a bit long are distasteful to him. This soul is so full of whatever it has just been doing or what it is going to do next, its boredom is so great, that this poor unfortunate thing is almost in agony. It is still alive, but it is not capable of doing anything to gain Heaven.[30]

Many of his early sermons also spoke against the obvious sins he saw in Ars: cursing, blaspheming, profaning the Lord's Day, gathering at taverns and engaging in immodest activities there. "The tavern is the devil's own shop, the school where Hell retails its dogmas, the market where souls are bartered, the place where families are broken up, where health is undermined, where quarrels are started and murders committed," he warned.[31]

By 1853, St. John Vianney had tried to run away from Ars four times to enter a monastery, but decided after the final attempt that monastic life was not God's will for him. He embraced his parish vocation of hearing confessions, saying Mass, and visiting parishioners, spending long hours in front of the Blessed Sacrament for sustenance. He delighted in teaching the catechism daily to the children of Ars. Soon, the adults attended as well, and he learned that many who were children during the Revolution did not know or truly understand the faith. He usually got only about two or three hours of sleep each night, and he often suffered attacks from the devil, who on one occasion even set fire to his bed.

"If a priest is determined not to lose his soul, so soon as any disorder arises in the parish, he must trample underfoot all human considerations as well as the fear of the contempt and hatred of his people. He must not allow anything to bar his way in the discharge of duty, even were he certain of being murdered on coming down from the pulpit," he said in a sermon.[32]

It took John Vianney about ten years to bring spiritual renewal to the small village, which was noticed by many in the surrounding villages. The people of Ars no longer worked on Sunday, drunkenness declined, and more and more people filled the church each year. Many taverns closed and domestic quarrels were greatly reduced. "Ars is no longer Ars," he wrote.

John Vianney believed in the idea of universal holiness. He taught that sanctity was a possibility that was open to all Christians. He read the lives of the saints and used them often as examples of those who became holy through personal sacrifice. "We must practice mortification. For this is the path which all the Saints have followed," he preached from the pulpit. "As long as we have no love in our hearts, we shall never be saints. To be a Christian and to live in sin is a monstrous contradiction. A Christian must be holy."

Tears frequently accompanied his preaching. He could never talk of sin and sinners without crying. He wept while making the Stations of the Cross or distributing the Eucharist. Especially toward the end of his life, he could never preach about the Eucharist, the goodness and love of God, or the happiness of heaven (his favorite topics), without being overwhelmed by his own tears.

On August 4, 1859, at age seventy-three, John Vianney died after being pastor in Ars for forty-one years. He was canonized on May 31, 1925. Today, more than five hundred thousand people visit Ars each year to see the incorrupt body of a great saint who devoted his life to the sacrament of Reconciliation and leading others on the path to holiness.

St. John Vianney's feast day is August 4.

St. John Vianney, pray for us that we may attain holiness.

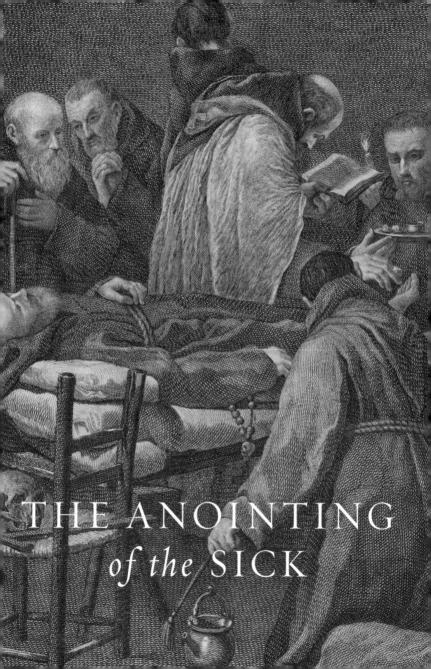

THE ANOINTING
of the SICK

THE ANOINTING *of the* SICK
St. Damien of Molokai

St. Damien of Molokai personified the sacrament of the Anointing of the Sick; he lived and died ministering spiritually and physically to the lepers on the island of Molokai, Hawaii. His sixteen-year commitment to their care was a visible sacrifice, culminating in the loss of his own life to the terrible disease. His mission was a literal fulfillment of Christ's words: "No one has greater love than this, to lay down one's life for one's friends" (John 15:13).

Born Jozef De Veuster in 1840, St. Damien grew up on a farm in rural Belgium and was the youngest of seven children. He followed three older siblings into religious life, joining the Congregation of the Sacred Hearts of Jesus and Mary, as his brother did before him. Prophetically, he took the religious name Damien in honor of a third-century physician and martyr who worked with St. Cosmas caring for the sick.

Brother Damien De Veuster practiced a daily devotion to St. Francis Xavier, asking that he too be sent out as a missionary. His older brother was ordered to go to Hawaii to serve there with the Sacred Heart priests, but he became ill, and Brother Damien volunteered to go in his place. The Sacred Heart superiors initially doubted that he had the education to become a priest, but Damien was intelligent and demonstrated his capability by quickly learning Latin from his brother. So his religious superiors relented and agreed to send him to Hawaii. Damien arrived on the Big Island in 1864 and was ordained a priest two months later. For nine years, he worked on the island as a priest, leading a normal and undistinguished pastoral life.

In 1866, Hawaiian King Kamehameha V established a leper colony on the Kalaupapa Peninsula on the island of Molokai, just off the coast of Maui, to quarantine the native population who had contracted the disease. Originating with the European explorers who had come upon the paradise of Hawaii, diseases such as smallpox, cholera, influenza, and tuberculosis would nearly wipe out the native people, who had no immunity to these foreign viruses. And one of the most brutal of these was leprosy, also called Hansen's disease.

Those with leprosy were simply dropped off and left to survive on their own on the desolate Kalaupapa Peninsula. Many were Catholic and asked for a priest, but the bishop initially denied their request, saying that it would be a "death sentence." Finally, in 1873, the bishop relented and four priests started to serve the people on a rotational basis. Damien became one of the chaplains that lived in Molokai for three months each year. Soon, Damien volunteered to remain there permanently in order to care continually for the people's physical, medical, and spiritual needs. His superior told him he could stay "as long as your devotion dictates."[33] That turned out to be the rest of his life.

"As long as the lepers can care for themselves," wrote the superintendent of the board of health, "they are comparatively comfortable, but as soon as the dreadful disease renders them helpless, it would seem that even demons themselves would pity their condition and hasten their death."[34]

For a long time, Fr. Damien was the only one committed to being there to support the colony, often called a "living graveyard."[35] One of the first things Fr. Damien did was to bring the consolations of the Catholic faith to the lepers facing death each day. He offered the sacrament of the Anointing of the Sick constantly. He celebrated funeral Masses and organized burials, teaching the Catholic view of death not as an end, but as a beginning of eternal life. He also administered the other sacraments and celebrated the Eucharist often. He preached, taught, and lived the healing and saving power of Jesus Christ.

Sometimes, indeed, I still feel some repugnance when I have to hear the confessions of those near their end, whose wounds are full of maggots. Often, also, I scarce know how to administer extreme unction [Anointing of the Sick], when both hands and feet are nothing but raw wounds. This may give you some idea of my daily work. Picture to yourself a collection of huts with eight hundred lepers. No doctor; in fact, as there is no cure, there seems no place for a doctor's skill.[36]

Fr. Damien went beyond spiritual care and did whatever was necessary. He dressed wounds, washed bodies, dug graves, and healed physical and emotional illness as best he could. Many patients had become severe alcoholics out of despair, making liquor from tree roots. Every kind of immorality and misbehavior was rampant in the lawless colony, including sexual immorality, violence, and drunkenness.

He filled the leadership void in the community, establishing rules of law and asking residents to unite to build houses, schools, and eventually the parish church, St. Philomena, which still stands on Molokai today. Employing his carpentry skills, he led the building efforts and even developed a water system. From his background on the family farm, he taught them how to grow crops to improve their food supply, which was meagerly provided by the Hawaiian government. Over the years, he became the leper colony's most effective advocate to obtain promised government support. In addition, he convinced the Franciscan Sisters of Syracuse, led by Mother Marianne Cope, to come and help care for the lepers.

Sadly, after twelve years of acting in the person of Christ for these people, Fr. Damien contracted leprosy. He realized he had the disease when he was bathing his feet and could not feel any warmth. Since the disease attacks the nerve endings, a lack of feeling is one of the common symptoms.

"I make myself a leper with the lepers to gain all to Jesus Christ,"[37] said Fr. Damien. For four years he continued his work, while the disease slowly took over his body. He often prayed the rosary in the cemetery and spent time in Eucharistic Adoration. "It is at the foot of the altar that we find the necessary strength in our isolation," he wrote.[38]

After sixteen years in the colony, Fr. Damien died on April 15, 1889. He was initially buried nearby, but then his remains were transferred to Belgium in 1936. His right hand was returned to Hawaii in 1995 to be reburied in his original grave at Molokai.

Although he never met Fr. Damien, Robert Louis Stevenson defended him against criticism from a Presbyterian minister:

It was [Fr. Damien's] part, by one striking act of martyrdom, to direct all men's eyes on that distressful country. At a blow, and with the price of his life, he made the place illustrious and public. And that, if you will consider largely, was the one reform needful . . . It brought money; it brought (best individual addition of them all) the sisters; it brought supervision, for public opinion and public interest landed with the man [Fr. Damien] . . . If ever any man brought reforms, and died to bring them, it was he."[39]

Damien was beatified by Pope John Paul II in Brussels, Belgium, in 1995, and canonized by Pope Benedict XVI on October 11, 2009. One of his canonization miracles was the disappearance of Audrey Toguchi's incurable cancer in May 1999. Toguchi had traveled to Molokai to pray at Damien's grave and to seek his intercession for her healing.

April 15, the day of his passing, is a minor statewide holiday in Hawaii. St. Damien is also the unofficial saint for many HIV/AIDS sufferers, in addition to being the patron of people with leprosy.

St. Damien's feast day is May 10.

St. Damien, pray for us in the midst of sickness and at the hour of our death. Amen.

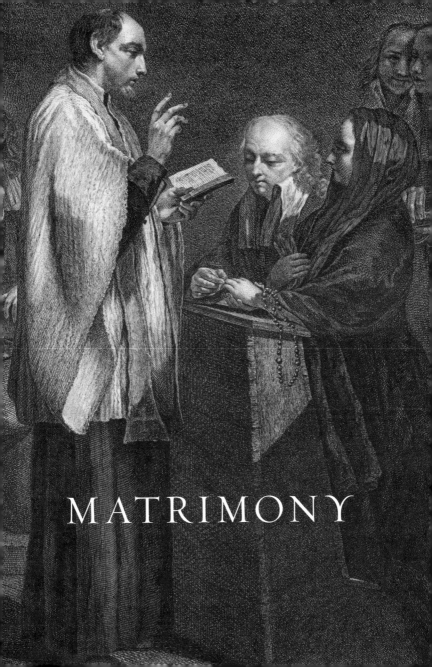

MATRIMONY

MATRIMONY
Sts. Louis and Zélie Martin

Beatified by Pope Benedict XVI in 2008 and canonized by Pope Francis in 2015, Sts. Louis and Zélie Martin are the first married couple with children to be canonized at the same time. They had nine children; three died in infancy and one died at the age of five. Their remaining five daughters all entered religious life, with the most famous being their youngest, St. Thérèse of Lisieux (the Little Flower). The Doctor of the Church is best known for her "little way": doing all things, no matter how small, with great love.

Louis and Zélie filled St Thérèse's childhood with the "little way" of love, so her deepest identity was learned in her family home. In her autobiography, *Story of a Soul*, St. Thérèse writes, "God was pleased all through my life to surround me with *love*, and the first memories I have are stamped with smiles and the most tender caresses."[40]

Louis Martin was born in 1823 in Bordeaux, France. Louis benefited from a very strong Catholic upbringing and also an education with the Brothers of Christian Schools. His father, a career military officer, was noted for his outstanding piety. At Mass, Captain Martin's soldiers were surprised to see him remain kneeling so long after the Consecration; when the chaplain related this story to him, Captain Martin quickly answered, "Tell them it is because I believe!" Louis did not follow his father into the military, but pursued watchmaking, which was more suited to his quiet nature and his great manual dexterity.

At twenty-two, Louis explored entering religious life at the Great Saint Bernard Hospice, where the monks dedicated themselves to prayer and to rescuing travelers stranded in the Alps. The Prior required that he complete his studies in Latin before entering the Novitiate. Louis tried to reengage his studies but was unsuccessful; with regret, he decided not to pursue his dream of religious life but to continue to work as a watchmaker. He lived in Alençon with his parents, working several jobs. His mother was on the look-out for a suitable wife for Louis, and she noticed a young woman in the lace-making school she attended who was very talented and respectable, also from a strongly religious family. The young woman was Zélie Guérin, born in Normandy in 1831, but now living in Alençon with her parents.

Like Louis, Zélie initially desired to enter religious life. When she applied to the Daughters of Charity, the Mother Superior told her that religious life was not God's will for her. Though saddened by the words of the Mother Superior, she was at the same time optimistic at the thought of a different vocation. She said, "I will enter the married state in order to fulfill Your holy will. I beg of You to give me many children and to let them all be consecrated to You."[41] On December 8, 1851, she received an inspiration from God: "See to the making of Point d'Alençon [Alençon lace]."[42] After attending a lace-making school, she set up her own lace-making shop.

One day, Zélie saw Louis as she was crossing a bridge and was impressed by his noble and dignified appearance. Then she heard an interior voice saying, "This is he whom I have prepared for you."[43] The two young people were introduced, quickly fell in love, and married only three months after their first meeting! At the wedding, Louis presented Zélie with a silver medallion engraved with the names "Tobias and Sarah," which represented his view of the upcoming marriage as one where the spouses would totally trust the Lord and submit to his will in everything, just as these biblical figures from the book of Tobit had done.

Still intrigued by the discipline and beauty of a religious vocation, Louis and Zélie decided to live together celibately as an expression of piety, following the example of St. Joseph and the Blessed Mother. For ten months, they prioritized the development of a spiritual communion, until their confessor convinced them that piety expresses itself in a different way within the sacrament of Matrimony—namely, by being "fruitful and multiplying." In the next thirteen years, Zélie gave birth to nine children (they took spiritual direction very well). Their pursuit of holiness changed in accordance with their vocation. In a letter to her oldest daughter, Zélie wrote:

> When we had our children, our ideas changed somewhat. Thenceforward we lived only for them; they made all our happiness and we would never have found it save in them. In fact, nothing any longer cost us anything; the world was no longer a burden to us. As for me, my children were my great compensation, so that I wished to have many in order to bring them up for Heaven.[44]

Louis and Zélie modeled their marriage after the love that Jesus gave to all humanity on the cross. They embraced the marriage bond as a strong, *sacrificial* love for each other, their children, and their neighbors. The Martin family lived modestly and reached out to the poor and the elderly, performing many works of mercy in their community.

As parents, they prayed daily with their children and taught them the faith by word and example. As an act of love toward Zélie, Louis gave up his watchmaking business to help Zélie manage and grow her lace business and care for their children, who were often ill. Louis represented her company in Paris, buying supplies to make lace and selling her artistic work in stores and to private clients. They were true partners in everything, with Christ always in their midst.

The Martins put their faith into action and demonstrated to the world around them the true meaning of marriage as a covenant by which "a man and a woman establish between themselves a partnership of the whole of life and which is ordered by its nature to the good of the spouses and the procreation and education of offspring."[45] They created a culture of seeking holiness in their home, and all five of their surviving daughters entered the convent. As Pope Francis said in his homily upon their canonization, "The holy spouses . . . practiced Christian service in the family, creating day by day an environment of faith and love which nurtured the vocations of their daughters."[46] In his homily at the Mass for their beatification, Cardinal José Saraiva Martins said, "Louis and Zélie understood that they could sanctify themselves not despite marriage but through, in, and by marriage, and that their nuptials would be considered as the starting point for a rising together."[47]

In 1877, at age forty-five, Zélie died of breast cancer after suffering greatly. Louis and his daughters moved to Lisieux to live near his brother and sister-in-law, who offered to help raise the girls. Gradually, his daughters left to enter the convent. Despite his loneliness, he said, "It is a great, great honor for me that the Good Lord desires to take all of my children. If I had anything better, I would not hesitate to offer it to him."[48] After suffering multiple strokes, he was admitted to a psychiatric hospital, where he spent three years. He was released into the care of his brother-in-law and daughters, and died in 1894. St. Thérèse would later write, "God gave me a father and a mother who were more worthy of heaven than of earth."[49]

The canonization of both Louis and Zélie Martin together spoke volumes about their personal holiness, but also spoke to the importance of marriage as a sacramental institution. Upholding the sanctity and necessity of marriage in a culture has "a very decisive bearing on the continuation of the human race, on the personal development and eternal destiny of the individual members of a family, and on the dignity, stability, peace, and prosperity of the family itself and of human society as a whole."[50]

Fr. Romano Gambalunga, OCD, the postulator for the cause of canonization, wrote, "It's the first time a couple have been canonized as a couple, and this is a beautiful sign for Christian families, who often are left without any support and have to go against the grain, especially in the West, to live and educate their children in the truth of creation and with that love that God has given us in Christ."[51]

It is fitting that both miracles required for their canonization concerned the mysterious healings of newborn babies with terminal ailments. The first, Pietro Schilirò, was born in Italy with a congenital lung deformation; the doctors said he could not survive. The priest who was called to baptize him encouraged his parents to pray for the Martins' intercession. Pietro is now a healthy young adult.

The second miracle concerned little Carmen, born prematurely at twenty-eight weeks in Spain. Two days later, she suffered a cerebral hemorrhage that caused near-fatal blood poisoning. Her parents went to the Carmelite nuns seeking guidance; the nuns suggested they pray for the intercession of the Martins, who had just been beatified a few days before. After being in critical condition, she experienced a complete cure, and was released on January 2, 2009, the 135th anniversary of the birth of the Martins' youngest daughter, St. Thérèse.

The Martins' feast day is July 12.

Sts. Louis and Zélie, pray for us and for all married couples to take their love and example into the public arena as a sign of God's love for all mankind.

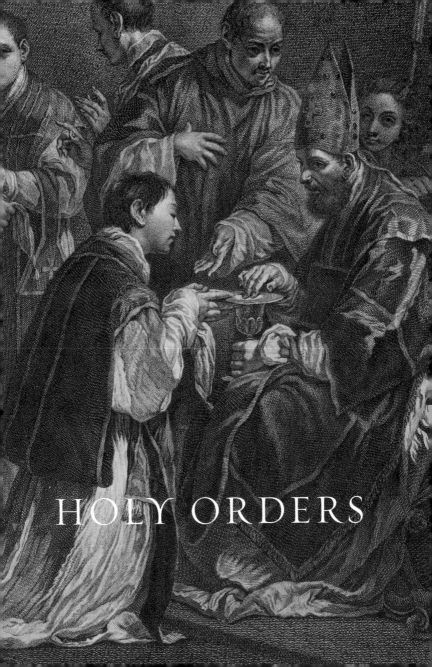

HOLY ORDERS

HOLY ORDERS
St. Maximilian Kolbe

All the baptized are called to embrace and live out the three offices of Christ: priest, prophet, and king. The ordained priest, however, serves out these roles uniquely through apostolic succession. Maximilian Kolbe, priest and saint, lived his calling in an exemplary and truly heroic fashion, which could only be fully appreciated after his death.

Born Raymond Kolbe in Russian-occupied Poland in 1894, he was the second son of a weaver. Being a normal young boy prone to mischief, he often received mild scoldings from his mother. After one such episode when he was ten, he asked the Blessed Mother, "Whatever will become of me." "Suddenly, to his surprise and wonderment, the Blessed Mother appeared before him in radiant beauty, her face full of tenderness and compassion. She held a crown in each hand, one white and the other red. The white crown stood for purity, and the red crown represented martyrdom. Mary asked Raymond to choose one.

After some thought, he answered with the zeal of a future saint, 'I choose both.' Pleased, the Blessed Mother smiled and then disappeared."[52]

Kolbe indeed became a priest and offered the sacraments throughout his life, even in the death camp at Auschwitz. Standing in the person of Christ, he became a ready victim and sacrificed his own life for a fellow prisoner. As prophet, he evangelized through his publishing company and founded the Militia Immaculata, or Army of Mary, to bring those who were the furthest from Christ into the Church through the intercession of the Virgin Mary. As king, he rightly ordered his monastic community and the Auschwitz bunkhouses to the right praise of God, showing by his quiet and non-violent manner that God could not be killed in the death camps.

His path to the priesthood began with his older brother by his side. Raymond and Francis were so determined to enter religious life that they traveled illegally from the Russian to the Austrian part of Poland in 1907 to enter the Conventual Franciscan junior seminary. Raymond entered the novitiate and took his first vows in 1911, adopting the name Maximilian, and his final vows in 1914, adding "Maria" to his name in honor of the Blessed Virgin.

Ordained in 1918, Maximilian Maria Kolbe also earned doctorates in philosophy and theology in Rome. While there, he founded the Militia Immaculata—also called the Army of Mary—to combat the Freemason movement and evangelize the enemies of the Catholic Church and all sinners through the intercession of the Blessed Mother. The Immaculata friars were early media evangelists, using modern printing techniques to publish catechetical and devotional texts, as well as a daily newspaper with a circulation of 230,000 and a monthly magazine with a circulation of over one million.

In 1919, Kolbe returned to liberated Poland and established the monastery of Niepokalanów (the "City of the Immaculata") near Warsaw, establishing a seminary, a radio station, and several other organizations, all united in promoting the veneration of the Virgin Mary. In the early thirties, he went on a series of mission trips to Japan, where he founded a monastery on a mountainside outside Nagasaki, a Japanese newspaper, and a seminary. His Nagasaki monastery escaped destruction by the atomic bomb and still stands today, contributing to the Japanese Catholic Church.

When the Nazis invaded Poland in 1939, Kolbe protected his brothers at the monastery by sending most of them home. The remaining brothers turned the monastery into a shelter for three thousand Polish refugees, most of them Jews, and shared all they had with them. The Germans seized and closed the friary in 1941 and sent Kolbe and four of his brothers to Auschwitz as a punishment for sheltering Jews.

In the inhumane environment of Auschwitz, Kolbe personified Christ constantly, never complaining and always reaching out to others with gentleness, comfort, and hope. He slept less than his bunkmates and spent the nights going from bed to bed, saying, "I am a Catholic priest. Can I do anything for you?" A prisoner recalled how he and others often crawled across the floor to be near Kolbe's bed in order make their confessions and receive consolation. Food was minimal and everyone clambered to get his share. Kolbe always stood aside and waited until all were served, often finding that there was no food left when it was his turn. Kolbe encouraged the prisoners to forgive the Nazis and to overcome evil with good. When beaten by the guards, Kolbe never cried out but instead prayed for his persecutors. The Auschwitz infirmary doctor, Rudolph Diem, later recalled, "I can say with certainty that during my four years there, I never saw such a sublime example of the love of God or one's neighbor."[53]

In July 1941, a man from Kolbe's bunker escaped from the camp. In retaliation, the guards selected ten men to die of starvation. One of the men selected, Franciszek Gajowniczek, cried in anguish, "Please, I have a wife and two children. I'll never see them again." Kolbe stepped forward and said, "I am a Catholic priest . . . I wish to take this man's place. I have no family. I am old and sick. He can do more work."[54] Dumbfounded, the guard accepted the substitution, and the ten were led to the starvation bunker. The pardoned prisoner, Gajowniczek, lived to see liberation from the camp and to witness the canonization of Fr. Maximilian Kolbe. He later recalled,

> I could only thank him with my eyes. I was stunned and could hardly grasp what was going on. The immensity of it: I, the condemned, am to live and someone else willingly and voluntarily offers his life for me—a stranger. Is this some dream?

> I was put back into my place without having had time to say anything to Maximilian Kolbe. I was saved. And I owe to him the fact that I could tell you all this. The news quickly spread all round the camp. It was the first and the last time that such an incident happened in the whole history of Auschwitz.[55]

Fr. Maximilian Kolbe stayed true to his vocation as priest, prophet, and king, even during the last days of a very painful death. After the liberation, Bruno Borgowiec, who was assigned to service the starvation bunker as a janitor, testified about Kolbe's last days:

> In the cell of the poor wretches there were daily loud prayers, the rosary and singing, in which prisoners from neighboring cells also joined. When no S.S. men were in the Block I went to the Bunker to talk to the men and comfort them. Fervent prayers and songs to the Holy Mother resounded in all the corridors of the Bunker. I had the impression I was in

a church. Fr Kolbe was leading and the prisoners responded in unison. They were often so deep in prayer that they did not even hear that inspecting S.S. men had descended to the Bunker; and the voices fell silent only at the loud yelling of their visitors. When the cells were opened the poor wretches cried loudly and begged for a piece of bread and for water, which they did not receive, however. If any of the stronger ones approached the door he was immediately kicked in the stomach by the S.S. men, so that falling backwards on the cement floor he was instantly killed; or he was shot to death . . . Fr Kolbe bore up bravely, he did not beg and did not complain but raised the spirits of the others. . . . Since they had grown very weak, prayers were now only whispered. At every inspection, when almost all the others were now lying on the floor, Fr Kolbe was seen kneeling or standing in the center as he looked cheerfully in the face of the S.S. men.[56]

At the end of two weeks, Fr. Kolbe and a few others were still alive and the cell was needed for other victims. So the Nazis gave them each an injection of carbolic acid. "Fr. Kolbe, with a prayer on his lips, himself gave his arm to the executioner. Unable to watch this, I left under the pretext of work to be done. Immediately after the S.S. men with the executioner had left I returned to the cell, where I found Fr. Kolbe leaning in a sitting position against the back wall with his eyes open and his head drooping sideways. His face was calm and radiant," Borgowiec recalled in awe.[57]

The story traveled like wildfire through Auschwitz. A survivor later declared that Kolbe's death, like Christ's, was "a shock filled with hope, bringing new life and strength. . . . It was like a powerful shaft of light in the darkness of the camp."[58] Fr. Dwight Longenecker commented:

Kolbe's death as a sacrificial victim somehow turned the tables as the death of every martyr turns the tables, and shows even at the moment of death that violence can never win. As the darkness can never overcome even the smallest light, so the hatred of hell can never overcome the love of heaven.

In the center of Kolbe's cell deep in the cellar of the punishment block the candles are a sign for they are Paschal candles. They stand like the three crosses on the hill—like three sentinels they stand alone in the unrelenting gloom of the harsh concrete room. Presented by two popes and a cardinal, the Paschal candles are solemn reminders that even in the darkest place there is hope, and that even in the depths of the extermination camps the life and light of Easter conquers all.[59]

St. Maximilian Kolbe's feast day is August 14.

St. Maximilian Kolbe, pray for us that we may be a beacon of light in the darkness of our world today.

BIBLIOGRAPHY

Francis Xavier

Bireley, Robert. "Francis Xavier." In *Encyclopedia Britannica Online*. December 24, 2019. https://www.britannica.com/biography/Saint-Francis-Xavier.

Broom, Ed. "Ten Lessons in Evangelization from St. Francis Xavier." Catholic Exchange. December 3, 2019, https://catholicexchange.com/ten-secrets-of-evangelization-from-st-francis-xavier.

Kosloski, Philip. "The Holy Hand that Baptized More than 700,000 People." Aleteia. December 3, 2017. https://aleteia.org/2017/12/03/the-holy-hand-that-baptized-more-than-700000-people/.

Lives of the Saints: With Excerpts from Their Writings. Introduction by Fr. Thomas Plassmann, OFM. New York: John J. Crawley & Co., Inc., 1954.

Mooney, Debra. "Who was Francis Xavier: A Modern View of His Life and Work." Xavier University, https://www.xavier.edu/mission-identity/xaviers-mission/who-is-francis-xavier.

John Paul II

Barron, Robert. *Catholicism: Journey to the Heart of the Faith*. New York: Image, 2011.

"Biographical Profile of John Paul II (1920–2005)." Vatican website. April 27, 2014. http://www.vatican.va/special/canonizzazione-27042014/documents/biografia_gpii_canonizzazione_en.html.

Blakemore, William. "St. John Paul II." In *Encyclopedia Britannica Online*. June 24, 2019. https://www.britannica.com/biography/Saint-John-Paul-II.

"John Paul II Biography." Biography. October 15, 2019. https://www.biography.com/religious-figure/john-paul-ii.

"Saint John Paul II." Catholic Online. Accessed March 9, 2020. https://www.catholic.org/saints/saint.php?saint_id=6996.

Clare of Assisi

Armstrong, Regis J., OFM Cap., editor and translator. *The Lady—Clare of Assisi: Early Documents*. New York: New City Press, 2006.

Dhont, Rene-Charles, OFM. *Clare Among Her Sisters*. St. Bonaventure, NY: Franciscan Institute Publications, 1987.

Thomas of Celano. *The Life of Saint Clare*. Philadelphia: Dolphin, 1910.

John Vianney

Otten, Susan Tracy. "St. Jean-Baptiste-Marie Vianney." *The Catholic Encyclopedia*. Vol. 8. New York: Robert Appleton Company, 1910. http://www.newadvent.org/cathen/08326c.htm.

"St. John Vianney." Catholic Online. Accessed March 9, 2020. https://www.catholic.org/saints/saint.php?saint_id=399.

"St. John Vianney." In *Encyclopedia Britannica Online*. July 31, 2019. https://www.britannica.com/biography/Saint-Jean-Baptiste-Marie-Vianney.

Trochu, Abbé François. *The Curé D'Ars: St. Jean-Marie-Baptiste Vianney.* Charlotte, NC: TAN Books, 2013.

Damien Molokai

Char, Sherie. "Hawaii's Father Damien: From Priesthood to Sainthood." *Hawai'i Magazine.* October 10, 2019. https://www.hawaiimagazine.com/blogs/hawaii_today/2009/10/10/Damien_Hawaii_Saint_Molokai_Kalaupapa_canonization.

"Saint Damien de Veuster of Moloka'i." Franciscan Media. Accessed March 9, 2020. https://www.franciscanmedia.org/saint-damien-de-veuster-of-moloka-i/.

"St. Damien of Molokai." Catholic Online. Accessed March 9, 2020. https://www.catholic.org/saints/saint.php?saint_id=2817.

"St. Damien of Molokai." In Encyclopedia Britannica Online. January 1, 2020. https://www.britannica.com/biography/Saint-Damien-of-Molokai.

"St. Father Damien of Molokai." Catholic Exchange. May 10, 2019. https://catholicexchange.com/blessed-father-damien-of-molokai.

Teeling, Bartle. "Father Damien." *The American Catholic Quarterly Review* 15, January to October, 1890.

Louis and Zélie Martin

LouisandZelieMartin.org

"Married Saints: Sts. Louis & Zelie Martin." For Your Marriage. Accessed March 9, 2020. https://www.foryourmarriage.org/married-saints-of-the-month-blessed-louis-zelie-martin/.

"Saints Louis Martin and Zélie Guerin." Franciscan Media. Accessed March 9, 2020. https://www.franciscanmedia.org/blesseds-louis-martin-and-zelie-guerin/.

St. Thérèse of Lisieux, *Story of a Soul*, trans. John Clarke, OCD. 3rd edition. Washington, DC: ICS Publications, 2017.

Maximilian Kolbe

Chenu, Bruno, Claude Prud'homme, France Quere, and Jean Claude Thomas. *The Book of Christian Martyrs*. London: SCM Press, 1990.

Craig, Mary. *Blessed Maximilian Kolbe: Priest Hero of a Death Camp*. London: Catholic Truth Society, 1973. https://www.ewtn.com/catholicism/library/st-maximilian-kolbe-priest-hero-of-a-death-camp-5602.

James, Manas Ranjan. "The Martyrdom of Fr. Maximilian Kolbe." In *Martyrs in the History of Christianity*, edited by Franklyn Balasundaram, Chapter 6. Delhi, IN: Indian Society for Promoting Christian Knowledge, 1997.

New Catholic Encyclopedia, Maximilian Kolbe by John P. Whalen

ENDNOTES

1 Quoted in "Who Was Francis Xavier? A Modern View of His Life and Work," Debra Mooney, Ph.D., Xavier University website, https://www.xavier.edu/mission-identity/xaviers-mission/who-is-francis-xavier.

2 Henry James Coleridge, *The Life and Letters of Saint Francis Xavier*, vol. 1, 2nd ed. (London: Burns and Oates, 1874).

3 Letter of Saint Francis Xavier to Saint Ignatius, Office of Readings: Second Reading, in *The Liturgy of the Hours*, vol. 1, *Advent Season—Christmas Season* (New York: Catholic Book Publishing Co., 1975), 1211.

4 *Catechism of the Catholic Church*, 2nd ed. (Washington, DC: USCCB Publishing, 2000), 330.

4 Bishop Robert Barron, *Catholicism: A Journey to the Heart of the Faith* (New York: Image, 2011), 151.

5 Pope John Paul II, Address at the World Youth Day Vigil of Prayer, Vatican website, August 19, 2000, http://w2.vatican.va/content/john-paul-ii/en/speeches/2000/jul-sep/documents/hf_jp-ii_spe_20000819_gmg-veglia.html.

6 Pope John Paul II, Address at the World Youth Day Evening Vigil, Vatican website, July 27, 2002, http://www.vatican.va/content/john-paul-ii/en/speeches/2002/july/documents/hf_jp-ii_spe_20020727_wyd-vigil-address.html.

7 Pope John Paul II, *Redemptoris Missio*, encyclical letter, Vatican website, December 7, 1990, http://www.vatican.va/content/john-paul-ii/en/encyclicals/documents/hf_jp-ii_enc_07121990_redemptoris-missio.html, no. 40.

8   Bishop Robert Barron, *Catholicism: A Journey to the Heart of the Faith* (New York: Image, 2011), 51.

9   Pope John Paul II, *Evangelium Vitae*, encyclical letter, Vatican website, March 25, 1995, http://www.vatican.va/content/john-paul-ii/en/encyclicals/documents/hf_jp-ii_enc_25031995_evangelium-vitae.html, no. 56.

11   Pope John Paul II, *Evangelium Vitae*, no. 28.

12   Pope John Paul II, *Fidei Depositum*, apostolic constitution, October 11, 1992, Vatican website, http://w2.vatican.va/content/john-paul-ii/en/apost_constitutions/documents/hf_jp-ii_apc_19921011_fidei-depositum.html.

13   Thomas of Celano, *The Life of Saint Clare* (Philadelphia: Dolphin, 1910), 37.

14   Regis J. Armstrong, OFM Cap., ed. and trans., *The Lady—Clare of Assisi: Early Documents* (New York: New City Press, 2006), 304.

15   Rene-Charles Dhont, OFM, *Clare Among Her Sisters* (St. Bonaventure, NY: Franciscan Institute Publications, 1987), 23.

16   Konferencja ascetyczne. Notatki sguchaczy przemówien Ojca Maksymiliana Kolbego (*Ascetical Conferences of Father Maximilian Kolbe from the notes of those who heard them*), Niepokalanow, December 18, 1938, quoted in Jerzy Domanski, *For the Life of the World: St. Maximilian and the Eucharist*, trans. Peter Fehlner, FI (Libertyville, IL: Academy of the Immaculate, 1993), 129.

17   Gli Scritti di Massimiliano Kolbe eroe di Oswiecim e beato della Chiesa (*The Writings of Maximilian Kolbe, Hero of Oswiecim and*

Blessed of the Church), vol. 3, 326, quoted in Domanski, *For the Life of the World*, 129.

18   Damien of Molokai to Rev. H.B. Chapman, August 26, 1886, in "The Apostle of the Lepers," *Donahoe's Magazine* 17 (January–July 1887): 34.

19   John Vianney, *The Little Catechism of the Curé of Ars: Selected Passages from the Writings of the Curé of Ars* (Charlotte, NC: TAN Books, 2011), Chapter 10, Kindle.

20   Thérèse of Lisieux, *Story of a Soul: The Autobiography of Saint Thérèse of Lisieux*, trans. John Clarke, OCD, 3rd ed. (Washington, DC: ICS Publications, 2017), 172.

21   Pope John Paul II, *Mane Nobiscum Domine*, apostolic letter, Vatican website, October 7, 2004, http://m.vatican.va/content/john-paul-ii/en/apost_letters/2004/documents/hf_jp-ii_apl_20041008_mane-nobiscum-domine.html, no. 18.

22   Pope John Paul II, *Message for World Mission Sunday 2004*, Vatican website, April 19, 2004, http://www.vatican.va/content/john-paul-ii/en/messages/missions/documents/hf_jp-ii_mes_20040429_world-day-for-missions-2004.html, no. 3.

23   *Mother Teresa: Essential Writings,* ed. Jean Maalouf (Maryknoll, NY: Orbis Books, 2001), 104.

24   Maria Faustina Kowalska, *Divine Mercy in My Soul: Diary of St. Maria Faustina Kowalska*, 2nd ed. (Stockbridge, MA: Marian Press, 1990), 45, no. 91.

25   Kowalska, *Divine Mercy in My Soul*, 494, no. 1385.

26   *Procès de l'Ordinaire*, 369, quoted in Abbé François Trochu, *The Curé D'Ars: St. Jean-Marie-Baptiste Vianney* (Charlotte, NC: TAN Books, 2013), 312.

27   *Memoire* of Abbe Marcel Gauthey, December 20, 1901, 3–6, quoted in Trochu, *Curé D'Ars*, 560–61.

28   *Procès de l'Ordinaire*, 1325, quoted in Trochu, *Curé D'Ars*, 454.

29   Trochu, *Curé D'Ars*, 454–55.

30   St. Jean-Marie Baptiste Vianney, *The Sermons of the Curé of Ars*, trans. Una Morrissey (Charlotte, NC: TAN Books, 2013), 9.

31   *Sermons*, t. III, 337, 334, 335, quoted in Trochu, *Curé D'Ars*, 148–9.

32   Sermons, Sur la colere, t. III, 352, quoted in Trochu, *Curé D'Ars*, 181.

33   "St. Damien of Molokai," EWTN online, https://www.ewtn.com/catholicism/saints/damien-of-molokai-539.

34   Libert Boeynaems, "Father Damien (Joseph de Veuster)," *The Catholic Encyclopedia*, vol. 4 (New York: Robert Appleton Company, 1908), http://www.newadvent.org/cathen/04615a.htm.

35   "St. Damien of Molokai," EWTN online.

36   Quoted in Bartle Teeling, "Father Damien," *The American Catholic Quarterly Review* 15 (January to October, 1890), 724.

37   Quoted in Bartle Teeling, "Father Damien," 725.

38 "Letter of Damien to Pamphile, Kohala, October 1867," *Le pere Damien De Veuster: Vie et documents*, compiled by Odile Van Gestel, SS.CC., quoted in Jan de Volder, *The Spirit of Father Damien: The Leper Priest—A Saint for Our Time* (San Francisco: Ignatius, 2010), 92.

39 Robert Louis Stevenson, *Father Damien: An Open Letter to the Reverend Doctor Hyde of Honolulu* (New York: Scribner's, 1916), 39.

40 St. Thérèse of Lisieux, *Story of a Soul*, trans. John Clarke, OCD, 3rd edition (Washington, DC: ICS Publications, 2017), 17.

41 Fr. Stephane-Joseph Piat, OFM, *The Story of a Family: The Home of St. Thérèse of Lisieux* (Charlotte, NC: TAN Books, 2015), 33.

42 Piat, *Story of a Family*, 33.

43 Piat, *Story of a Family*, 40.

44 Piat, *Story of a Family*, 48.

45 *Code of Canon Law*, c. 1055, § 1, Vatican website, http://www.vatican.va/archive/ENG1104/__P3V.HTM.

46 Pope Francis, Homily for the Canonization of Vincent Grossi, Mary of the Immaculate Conception, and Louis Martin and Marie-Azélie Guerin, October 18, 2015, Vatican website, http://www.vatican.va/content/francesco/en/homilies/2015/documents/papa-francesco_20151018_omelia-canonizzazioni.html.

47 Cardinal José Saraiva Martins, Homily at the Beatification of Louis and Zélie Martin, Carmel of Saint Joseph, https://www.stlouiscarmel.com/resources/homily-at-beatification-of-louis-and-zelie-martin/.

48 Ferdinand Holböck, *Married Saints and Blesseds: Through the Centuries* (San Francisco: Ignatius, 2002), 411.

49   Piat, *Story of a Family*, 426.

50   Second Vatican Council, *Gaudium et Spes*, pastoral constitution, Vatican website, December 7, 1965, http://www.vatican.va/archive/hist_councils/ii_vatican_council/documents/vat-ii_const_19651207_gaudium-et-spes_en.html.

51   "Married Couple is the 1st in Modern Times to Become Saints," *Los Angeles Times*, October 18, 2015, https://www.latimes.com/nation/ct-pope-married-couple-saints-20151018-story.html.

52   William LaMay, *The Life of St. Maximilian Kolbe: Apostle of Mass Communications* (self-pub., 2019), 16.

53   Elaine Murray Stone, *Maximilian Kolbe: Saint of Auschwitz* (Mahwah, NJ: Paulist Press, 1997), 80.

54   Stone, *Maximilian Kolbe*, 83.

55   Tejvan Pettinger, "Maximilian Kolbe Biography," Biography Online, August 3, 2014, https://www.biographyonline.net/spiritual/maximilian-kolbe.html.

56   Mary Craig, *Blessed Maximilian Kolbe: Priest Hero of a Death Camp* (London: Catholic Truth Society, 1973), https://www.ewtn.com/catholicism/library/st-maximilian-kolbe-priest-hero-of-a-death-camp-5602.

57   Craig, *Blessed Maximilian Kolbe*.

58   Craig, *Blessed Maximilian Kolbe*.

59   Fr. Dwight Longenecker, "Maximilian Kolbe and the Redemption of Auschwitz," Aleteia, April 28, 2016, https://aleteia.org/2016/04/28/maximilian-kolbe-and-the-redemption-of-auschwitz/2/.